Footprints on Mommy's Heart

Mary Ann Vitale

Art by: Sachin S. Modgekar

Edited by: Sisa Colletti Vanelli

First Published by Bookshelf Publishing 10/11/2019

©2019 Mary Ann Vitale. All Rights Reserved.

Footprints on Mommy's Heart

ISBN: 978-1-7341211-0-0

This book is a work of fiction. People, places, events, and situations are the product of the author's imagination. Any resemblance to actual persons, living or dead, or historical events, is purely coincidental.

Printed in the United States of America

No part of this book may be reproduced, stored in a retrieval system, or transmitted by any means without the written permission of the author.

I would like to dedicate this book to God and my family, especially my grandchildren: Arabella, Karlina, Lincoln, Mason, Eric, Shaeahn, Glenn IV, Owen and Nolan.

Hello! My name is Arabella, but everybody calls me, "Bella."
My dad has a special name for me, "Peanut," because I am very small.
I am only two years old, but Grandma says, I am "two going on ten."
Whatever that means!

I have an older sister named Karlina, but I always call her "Keena."
I love to leave footprints all over, and she loves to leave fingerprints all over.
She even has her own book, *Fingerprints on the Mirror*, made by Grandma.
She is so lucky!

I will tell you a little secret in your ear, just like I tell Mommy.
I am a little jealous. I, also, want a book about my footprints.
Well, maybe I am a lot jealous. So I give Grandma a pen and paper.
She will not have a choice. She will make a footprint book for me!
Then, my sister and I will have a fingerprint and footprint book for you!

My little feet tiptoe on Mommy's heart,

And I trace my footprints with markers.

Mom will hang my picture on the wall

So she can look at my great work forever.

I love my footprints on Mommy's heart!

I am the greatest artist!

I dance in the rain with my mouth wide open.

I hope to catch a raindrop on my tongue.

Then I jump in the puddles of water

And stomp my feet on the cement.

"Wow! Come and join the fun, Mom!

Look at my wet footprints!"

I go outside and step in the mud.

It's hard to resist. Swish, swish, swish,

The soft mud gushes over my toes.

Then I walk back inside my clean house

And track muddy footprints on the floor.

What a nice present for Mommy!

I like to take a shower with Mommy

And step out wrapped in a towel.

And, whoosh, our feet touch the soft mat.

I point out, "Look at our footprints, Mommy!

Yours are big! Mine are small!"

She looks at me and smiles!

With dirty feet, I stand by my cat

And pet the little kitty on his neck.

He leaves his paw prints on the floor,

And I compare them with my footprints.

"Mine are bigger! Please, don't cry, little kitty!

Let's go to sleep. You will feel better!"

Mom looks at us with love!

I love to play on the kitchen floor.

I dust it with flour and step all over.

I will make a new dance for Mommy

And show her my messy footprints.

Oops, I don't see them anymore!

"Mom, where did they go?"

I love to play with soft play dough

And make pizza, cakes, rings and flowers.

Today, I am going to make something new.

Barefooted, I leave footprints on the putty.

I wonder if Mom will love them!

I hope she keeps them!

I love to walk on the beach with Keena,

And leave behind our footprints on the sand.

We turn around to look, before they disappear.

Keena's look like Big Foot and mine like a small peanut!

I have to eat more, so I can grow big like Keena.

"Mom, give me more food to eat please!"

I dream of being in the zoo with a big lion,

After watching a movie with Mommy and Keena.

The lion pretends to be the "King of the jungle!"

He doesn't know that I am "Princess Arabella!"

I look at the lion's paw prints and my footprints.

Mine are better! The lion is jealous and roars!

"Run, Arabella, run! Mommy, save me!"

I help Mom fix her pretty bed.

She makes sure the covers are smooth.

I climb on the bed and set up the pillows.

It looks too perfect! So, I jump on the bed

Up and down like a monkey and yell "ta-da!"

Here is the new "Bella's Footprints Cover!"

"I made it just for you, Mommy!"

Hey, guys! I am not finished, yet!

One day, I will go to school

To become a nurse or doctor.

My feet will make new footprints,

Some small like a little birdie,

And some big like a giant dinosaur.

I plan to leave my mark in this big world!

Just like Keena, I have my own book.
She has Fingerprints on the Mirror,
And I have Footprints on Mommy's Heart.
Will Mommy love my book more than Keena's?
Fingerprints on the mirror can always be wiped out,
But, footprints on Mommy's heart can never be taken out!
"Now, don't get jealous, Keena!"

The End

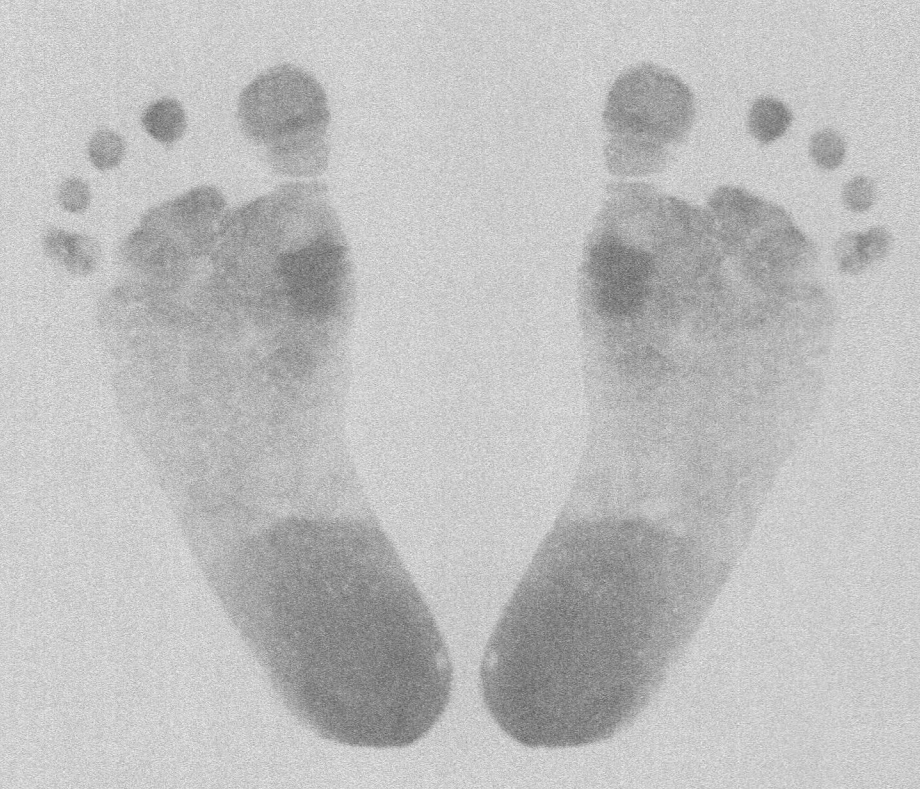

Mary Ann Vitale
To contact the author: www.facebook.com/maryann.vitale.9
or www.maryannvitaleauthor.blogspot.com

    Mary Ann Manzella Vitale was born in Cinisi, Sicily. She is a U. S. citizen who resides in Woodhaven, Michigan. She is married and has three children and many grandchildren. God has blessed her with the gift of writing children's stories in many languages. Mary Ann was inspired to write by her granddaughter, experiencing life through her eyes. This book and future stories by this talented author are sure to become children's favorites for many years to come.

Turn to the following page to see all of
Mary Ann Vitale's published books.

The Water Lily Fairy - 2013 YATR Award Winner

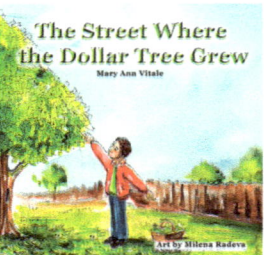
The Street Where the Dollar Tree Grew - 2014 LSOR Award Winner

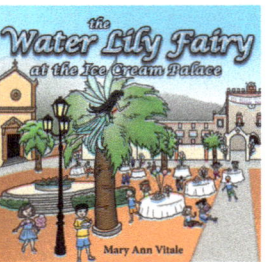
The Water Lily Fairy at the Ice Cream Palace

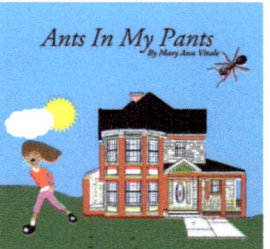
Ants In My Pants

Julie and Her Seven Calves

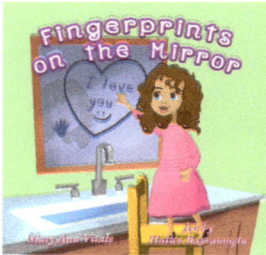
Fingerprints on the Mirror - 2017 Golden Book Award Reader's Choice Semifinalist

Mommy, Where Does Tiger Live?

Mouse Goes to the Doctor

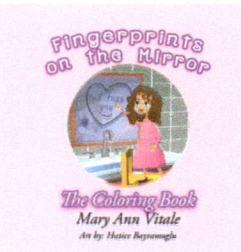
Fingerprints on the Mirror The Coloring Book

The Water Lily Fairy The Coloring Book

La Fata delle Ninfee

La Fata delle Ninfee al Castello del Gelato

Formiche Sui Miei Jeans

Hidden Treasures in a Book Vol. 1

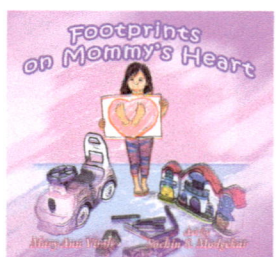
Footprints on Mommy's Heart

Click on the link: www.amazon.com/author/maryannvitale

You can purchase these books at Amazon, B&N, Author House, Walmart and worldwide.
Enjoy reading this book? Reviews are greatly appreciated.

www.ingramcontent.com/pod-product-compliance
Lightning Source LLC
Chambersburg PA
CBHW061134070526
44584CB00033B/4324